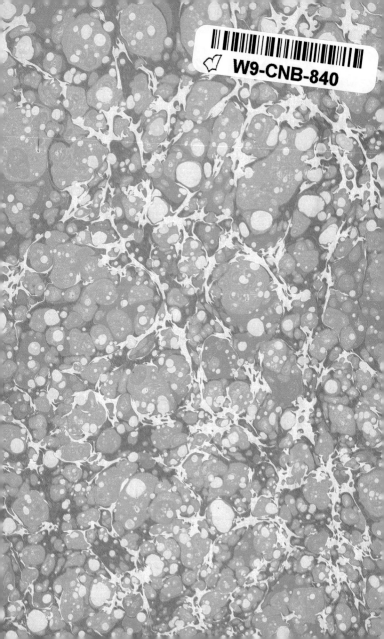

THE ILLUSTRATED POETS

THE ILLUSTRATED POETS
William Blake

Selected and with an introduction
by Peter Porter

OXFORD UNIVERSITY PRESS
1986

Oxford University Press, Walton Street, Oxford OX2 6DP

Oxford   New York   Toronto
Delhi   Bombay   Calcutta   Madras   Karachi
Kuala Lumpur   Singapore   Hong Kong   Tokyo
Nairobi   Dar es Salaam   Cape Town
Melbourne   Auckland
and associated companies in
Beirut   Berlin   Ibadan   Nicosia

Oxford is a trade mark of Oxford University Press

First published 1986 by Oxford University Press

British Library Cataloguing in Publication Data
Blake, William, *1757–1827*
William Blake.—(The illustrated poets)
I. Title II. Porter, Peter III. Series
821'.7 PR4142
ISBN 0-19-214166-X

Designed and produced by Aurum Press Limited,
33 Museum Street, London WC1A 1LD

Picture research by Juliet Brightmore

Typeset by Filmtype Services Ltd, Scarborough

Printed in Belgium by Proost

CONTENTS

INTRODUCTION

Blake's genius is like nobody else's in English litera-
ture. It is not just a matter of his inventing his own
theology, or peopling his Prophetic Books with spirits
and characters of an outlandish sort, it is his whole
way of looking at the world. The words which Samuel
Johnson applied to Blake's predecessor, the clinically
insane but religiously inspired poet, Christopher Smart,
apply also to Blake. Dr Johnson told Boswell that
'madness frequently discovers itself merely by un-
necessary deviation from the usual modes of the world.'
Smart was sent to Bedlam for carrying his deviation to
the lengths of waylaying strangers and urging them to
pray with him in public. Blake kept out of the mad-
house because he confined his religious and prophetic
enthusiasm to his poetry and his painting. Even so, he
was nearly in great trouble, being brought before the
magistrates for alleged sedition in 1804 when Britain
was in a crucial stage of her struggle with Revolution-
ary France. Blake was acquitted, but his writings were
eloquently on the side of revolution. Had he not been
a visionary genius, he might well have been a Jacobin
or a follower of Tom Paine. And Blake, unlike Smart,
was unorthodox in his whole approach to Christianity.

These matters may seem a long way off today, when
Blake is read and loved throughout the English-speak-
ing world, and in most other languages as well. His
status as chief prophet and guide to the 'Flower
Children' and 'hippies' of the sixties, however, tells us
much about his abiding excitement as an original and
inspiring writer. Put simply, William Blake's poetry
offers the reader a way through the daunting thickets

of religious dogma and establishment orthodoxy to the idea of personal revelation, to an intense experience of life perceived by our senses and our understanding. However, the pure essence of Blake the poet (a considerable amount of which is contained in this small book) is not the same as the full body of his writings. These are voluminous, and consist of books of inspirational poetry, largely shaped by his reading of the Old Testament and the mystical Protestants. Blake was self-educated and self-inspired. His Prophetic Books – *The Book of Thel*, *The Vision of the Daughters of Albion*, *The Marriage of Heaven and Hell*, *America*, *Europe*, *Vala*, *Milton* and *Jerusalem* – are today read only by devoted Blakeans and scholars. They can be impressive, especially if intoned by fine voices in antiphonal performance. But they are not what has made Blake loved and quoted throughout the world. Blake is *par excellence* a proverbial writer, a coiner of wonderfully illuminating sentences and phrases about the human condition whose truth we recognize, whether we acknowledge much else which he thought was true. And he did not hesitate to contradict himself, so that his poetry, like Shakespeare's, has the authority of an oracle. As he wrote: 'Hear the Voice of the Bard'. It is the voice of Innocence and Experience combined.

One further consideration separates Blake from other great poets in the English pantheon – his life's work as a painter and engraver. It is rare in any country to encounter an artist equally gifted in two disparate media. Blake's loyalty to the drawn image was even greater than his devotion to poetry and inspired literary utterance. He worked at his illustrations to the very end of his life, his rate of output increasing in old age. Most of his finest poems, on the other hand, belong to his early and middle years.

William Blake was born in Broad Street, London, in 1757, and, apart from an influential two-year period at the turn of the new century when he lived in Felpham, Sussex, he resided and worked in the capital all his life. He was trained as an engraver and worked at the craft (together with illustrating in watercolour) until his death in 1827. When not ten years old he saw visions of angels, and these visionary powers remained with him into maturity. Some idea of Blake's utterly original sense of mysticism can be gained from 'The Marriage of Heaven and Hell', in which he describes matter-of-factly the angels who prophesy to him. He observes that angels have tempers and can change colour at will. Throughout his writings, the extra-terrestrial is presented as naturally as the observably real.

This selection of Blake centres on his most pithy and concentrated work. His greatest lyrics, from 'The Songs of Innocence and Experience', are well represented and his proverbial utterance is emphasized. Since many of Blake's illustrations to his own works are little more than marginal embellishments, more complete and finished pictures have here been preferred.

The Ecchoing Green

The Sun does arise,
And make happy the skies;
The merry bells ring
To welcome the Spring;
The sky-lark and thrush,
The birds of the bush,
Sing louder around
To the bells' chearful sound,
While our sports shall be seen
On the Ecchoing Green.

Old John, with white hair,
Does laugh away care,
Sitting under the oak,
Among the old folk.
They laugh at our play,
And soon they all say:
'Such, such were the joys
'When we all girls & boys,
'In our youth-time were seen,
'On the Ecchoing Green.'

Till the little ones, weary,
No more can be merry;
The sun does descend,
And our sports have an end.
Round the laps of their mothers
Many sisters and brothers,
Like birds in their nest,
Are ready for rest,
And sport no more seen
On the darkening Green.

The Little Black Boy

My mother bore me in the southern wild,
And I am black, but O! my soul is white;
White as an angel is the English child,
But I am black as if bereav'd of light.

My mother taught me underneath a tree,
And sitting down before the heat of day,
She took me on her lap and kissed me,
And pointing to the east began to say:

'Look on the rising sun: there God does live,
'And gives his light, and gives his heat away;
'And flowers and trees and beasts and men recieve
'Comfort in morning, joy in the noon day.

'And we are put on earth a little space,
'That we may learn to bear the beams of love;
'And these black bodies and this sunburnt face
'Is but a cloud, and like a shady grove.

SONGS
OF
Innocence

The Author & Printer W Blake

'For when our souls have learn'd the heat to bear,
'The cloud will vanish; we shall hear his voice,
'Saying: "Come out from the grove, my love & care,
' "And round my golden tent like lambs rejoice".'

Thus did my mother say, and kissed me;
And thus I say to little English boy:
When I from black and he from white cloud free,
And round the tent of God like lambs we joy,

I'll shade him from the heat, till he can bear
To lean in joy upon our father's knee;
And then I'll stand and stroke his silver hair,
And be like him, and he will then love me.

The Chimney Sweeper

When my mother died I was very young,
And my father sold me while yet my tongue
Could scarcely cry ' 'weep! 'weep! 'weep! 'weep!'
So your chimneys I sweep, & in soot I sleep.

There's little Tom Dacre, who cried when his head,
That curl'd like a lamb's back, was shav'd, so I said
'Hush, Tom! never mind it, for when your head's bare
'You know that the soot cannot spoil your white hair.'

And so he was quiet, & that very night,
As Tom was a-sleeping, he had such a sight!
That thousands of sweepers, Dick, Joe, Ned & Jack,
Were all of them lock'd up in coffins of black.

And by came an Angel who had a bright key,
And he open'd the coffins & set them all free;
Then down a green plain leaping, laughing, they run,
And wash in a river, and shine in the Sun.

Then naked & white, all their bags left behind,
They rise upon clouds, and sport in the wind;
And the Angel told Tom, if he'd be a good boy,
He'd have God for his father, & never want joy.

And so Tom awoke; and we rose in the dark,
And got with our bags & our brushes to work.
Tho' the morning was cold, Tom was happy & warm;
So if all do their duty, they need not fear harm.

Spring

Sound the Flute!
Now it's mute.
Birds delight
Day and Night;
Nightingale
In the dale,
Lark in Sky,
Merrily,
Merrily, Merrily, to welcome in the Year.

Little Boy,
Full of joy;
Little Girl,
Sweet and small;
Cock does crow,
So do you;
Merry voice,
Infant noise,
Merrily, Merrily, to welcome in the Year.

Little Lamb,
Here I am;
Come and lick,
My white neck;
Let me pull
Your soft Wool;
Let me kiss
Your soft face:
Merrily, Merrily, we welcome in the Year.

Spring

Sound the Flute!
Now it's mute.
Birds delight
Day and Night.
Nightingale
In the dale
Lark in Sky
Merrily
Merrily Merrily to welcome in the Year

Little Boy
Full of joy.

Little

Nurse's Song

When the voices of children are heard on the green
And laughing is heard on the hill,
My heart is at rest within my breast
And everything else is still.

'Then come home, my children, the sun is gone down
'And the dews of night arise;
'Come, come, leave off play, and let us away
'Till the morning appears in the skies.'

'No, no, let us play, for it is yet day
'And we cannot go to sleep;
'Besides, in the sky the little birds fly
'And the hills are all covered with sheep.'

'Well, well, go & play till the light fades away
'And then go home to bed.'
The little ones leaped & shouted & laugh'd
And all the hills ecchoed.

The Divine Image

To Mercy, Pity, Peace and Love
All pray in their distress;
And to these virtues of delight
Return their thankfulness.

For Mercy, Pity, Peace and Love
Is God, our father dear,
And Mercy, Pity, Peace and Love
Is Man, his child and care.

For Mercy has a human heart,
Pity, a human face:
And Love, the human form divine,
And Peace, the human dress.

Then every man, of every clime,
That prays in his distress,
Prays to the human form divine,
Love, Mercy, Pity, Peace.

And all must love the human form,
In heathen, turk or jew.
Where Mercy, Love & Pity dwell
There God is dwelling too.

The Clod & the Pebble

'Love seeketh not Itself to please,
'Nor for itself hath any care;
'But for another gives its ease,
'And builds a Heaven in Hell's despair.'

So sang a little Clod of Clay,
Trodden with the cattle's feet:
But a Pebble of the brook
Warbled out these metres meet:

'Love seeketh only Self to please,
'To bind another to its delight;
'Joys in another's loss of ease,
'And builds a Hell in Heaven's despite.'

The Fly

Little Fly,
Thy summer's play
My thoughtless hand
Has brush'd away.

Am not I
A fly like thee?
Or art not thou
A man like me?

For I dance,
And drink, & sing;
Till some blind hand
Shall brush my wing.

If thought is life
And strength & breath,
And the want
Of thought is death;

Then am I
A happy fly,
If I live
Or if I die.

The Garden of Love

I went to the Garden of Love,
And saw what I never had seen:
A Chapel was built in the midst,
Where I used to play on the green.

And the gates of this Chapel were shut,
And 'Thou shalt not' writ over the door;
So I turn'd to the Garden of Love,
That so many sweet flowers bore;

And I saw it was filled with graves,
And tomb-stones where flowers should be;
And Priests in black gowns were walking their rounds,
And binding with briars, my joys & desires.

Ah! Sun-flower

Ah Sun-flower! weary of time,
Who countest the steps of the Sun,
Seeking after that sweet golden clime
Where the traveller's journey is done:

Where the Youth pined away with desire,
And the pale Virgin shrouded in snow
Arise from their graves and aspire
Where my Sun-flower wishes to go.

The Tyger

Tyger! Tyger! burning bright
In the forests of the night,
What immortal hand or eye
Could frame thy fearful symmetry?

In what distant deeps or skies
Burnt the fire of thine eyes?
On what wings dare he aspire?
What the hand dare sieze the fire?

And what shoulder, & what art,
Could twist the sinews of thy heart?
And when thy heart began to beat,
What dread hand? & what dread feet?

What the hammer, what the chain?
In what furnace was thy brain?
What the anvil, what dread grasp
Dare its deadly terrors clasp?

When the stars threw down their spears,
And water'd heaven with their tears,
Did he smile his work to see?
Did he who made the Lamb make thee?

Tyger! Tyger! burning bright
In the forests of the night,
What immortal hand or eye
Dare frame thy fearful symmetry?

The Tyger.

Tyger Tyger. burning bright,
In the forests of the night;
What immortal hand or eye.
Could frame thy fearful symmetry?

In what distant deeps or skies.
Burnt the fire of thine eyes?
On what wings dare he aspire?
What the hand, dare sieze the fire?

And what shoulder, & what art,
Could twist the sinews of thy heart?
And when thy heart began to beat,
What dread hand? & what dread feet?

What the hammer? what the chain,
In what furnace was thy brain?
What the anvil? what dread grasp,
Dare its deadly terrors clasp?

When the stars threw down their spears
And water'd heaven with their tears:
Did he smile his work to see?
Did he who made the Lamb make thee?

Tyger Tyger burning bright,
In the forests of the night:
What immortal hand or eye,
Dare frame thy fearful symmetry?

The Human Abstract

Pity would be no more
If we did not make somebody Poor;
And Mercy no more could be
If all were as happy as we.

And mutual fear brings peace,
Till the selfish loves increase:
Then Cruelty knits a snare,
And spreads his baits with care.

He sits down with holy fears,
And waters the ground with tears;
Then Humility takes its root
Underneath his foot.

Soon spreads the dismal shade
Of Mystery over his head;
And the Catterpiller and Fly
Feed on the Mystery.

And it bears the fruit of Deceit,
Ruddy and sweet to eat;
And the Raven his nest has made
In its thickest shade.

The Gods of the earth and sea
Sought thro' Nature to find this Tree;
But their search was all in vain:
There grows one in the Human Brain.

London

I wander thro' each charter'd street,
Near where the charter'd Thames does flow,
And mark in every face I meet
Marks of weakness, marks of woe.

In every cry of every Man,
In every Infant's cry of fear,
In every voice, in every ban,
The mind-forg'd manacles I hear.

How the Chimney-sweeper's cry
Every black'ning Church appalls;
And the hapless Soldier's sigh
Runs in blood down Palace walls.

But most thro' midnight streets I hear
How the youthful Harlot's curse
Blasts the new-born Infant's tear,
And blights with plagues the Marriage hearse.

A POISON TREE.

I was angry with my friend;
I told my wrath, my wrath did end.
I was angry with my foe:
I told it not, my wrath did grow.

And I waterd it in fears,
Night & morning with my tears:
And I sunned it with smiles,
And with soft deceitful wiles.

And it grew both day and night,
Till it bore an apple bright.
And my foe beheld it shine,
And he knew that it was mine.

And into my garden stole,
When the night had veild the pole;
In the morning glad I see,
My foe outstretchd beneath the tree.

A Poison Tree

I was angry with my friend:
I told my wrath, my wrath did end.
I was angry with my foe:
I told it not, my wrath did grow.

And I watered it in fears,
Night & morning with my tears;
And I sunned it with smiles,
And with soft deceitful wiles.

And it grew both day and night,
Till it bore an apple bright;
And my foe beheld it shine,
And he knew that it was mine,

And into my garden stole
When the night had veil'd the pole:
In the morning glad I see
My foe outstretch'd beneath the tree.

To Tirzah

Whate'er is Born of Mortal Birth
Must be consumed with the Earth
To rise from Generation free:
Then what have I to do with thee?

The Sexes sprung from Shame & Pride,
Blow'd in the morn; in evening died;
But Mercy chang'd Death into Sleep;
The Sexes rose to work & weep.

Thou, Mother of my Mortal part,
With cruelty didst mould my Heart,
And with false self-deceiving tears
Didst bind my Nostrils, Eyes & Ears:

Didst close my Tongue in senseless clay,
And me to Mortal Life betray.
The Death of Jesus set me free:
Then what have I to do with thee?

Proverbs of Hell

In seed time learn, in harvest teach, in winter enjoy.

Drive your cart and your plow over the bones of the dead.

The road of excess leads to the palace of wisdom.

Prudence is a rich, ugly old maid courted by Incapacity.

He who desires but acts not, breeds pestilence.

The cut worm forgives the plow.

Dip him in the river who loves water.

A fool sees not the same tree that a wise man sees.

He whose face gives no light, shall never become a star.

Eternity is in love with the productions of time.

The busy bee has no time for sorrow.

The hours of folly are measur'd by the clock, but of wisdom: no clock can measure.

All wholesome food is caught without a net or a trap.

Bring out number, weight & measure in a year of dearth.

No bird soars too high if he soars with his own wings.

A dead body revenges not injuries.

Proverbs of Hell

The head Sublime, the heart Pathos, the genitals Beauty,
   the hands & feet Proportion.

As the air to a bird or the sea to a fish, so is contempt
   to the contemptible.

The crow wish'd every thing was black, the owl, that eve-
   -ry thing was white.

Exuberance is Beauty.

If the lion was advised by the fox, he would be cunning.

Improvent makes strait roads, but the crooked roads
   without Improvement, are roads of Genius.

Sooner murder an infant in its cradle than nurse unact-
   -ed desires

Where man is not nature is barren.

Truth can never be told so as to be understood, and
   not be believd.

Enough! or Too much

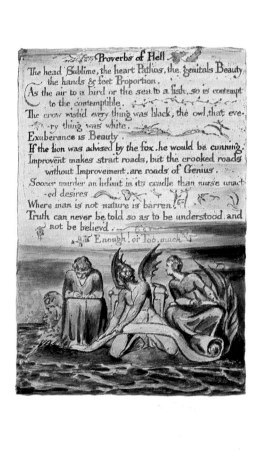

Christ at Prayer
(Parisi)

Father . . . not what I will but what You will.

Matt 26:39

The most sublime act is to set another before you.

If the fool would persist in his folly he would become wise.

Folly is the cloke of knavery.

Shame is Pride's cloke.

Prisons are built with stones of Law, Brothels with bricks of Religion.

The pride of the peacock is the glory of God.

The lust of the goat is the bounty of God.

The wrath of the lion is the wisdom of God.

The nakedness of woman is the work of God.

Excess of sorrow laughs: excess of joy weeps.

The roaring of lions, the howling of wolves, the raging of the stormy sea, and the destructive sword are portions of eternity too great for the eye of man.

The fox condemns the trap, not himself.

Joys impregnate, sorrows bring forth.

Let man wear the fell of the lion, woman the fleece of the sheep.

The bird a nest, the spider a web, man friendship.

The selfish smiling fool & the sullen frowning fool shall be both thought wise that they may be a rod.

What is now proved was once only imagin'd.

The rat, the mouse, the fox, the rabbet watch the
    roots; the lion, the tyger, the horse, the elephant
    watch the fruits.

The cistern contains: the fountain overflows.

One thought fills immensity.

Always be ready to speak your mind, and a base man
    will avoid you.

Every thing possible to be believ'd is an image of truth.

The eagle never lost so much time as when he
    submitted to learn of the crow.

The fox provides for himself but God provides for
    the lion.

Think in the morning, Act in the noon, Eat in the
    evening, Sleep in the night.

He who has suffer'd you to impose on him knows you.

As the plow follows words, so God rewards prayers.

The tygers of wrath are wiser than the horses of
    instruction.

Expect poison from the standing water.

You never know what is enough unless you know
    what is more than enough.

Listen to the fool's reproach! it is a kingly title!

The eyes of fire, the nostrils of air, the mouth of water, the beard of earth.

The weak in courage is strong in cunning.

The apple tree never asks the beech how he shall grow, nor the lion, the horse, how he shall take his prey.

The thankful reciever bears a plentiful harvest.

If others had not been foolish, we should be so.

The soul of sweet delight can never be defil'd.

When thou seest an Eagle, thou seest a portion of Genius: lift up thy head!

As the catterpiller chooses the fairest leaves to lay her eggs on, so the priest lays his curse on the fairest joys.

To create a little flower is the labour of ages.

Damn braces: Bless relaxes.

The best wine is the oldest, the best water the newest.

Prayers plow not! Praises reap not!
Joys laugh not! Sorrows weep not!

The head Sublime, the heart Pathos, the genitals Beauty, the hands & feet Proportion.

As the air to a bird or the sea to a fish, so is contempt to the contemptible.

The crow wish'd everything was black, the owl, that everything was white.

Exuberance is Beauty.

If the lion was advis'd by the fox he would be cunning.

Improvement makes strait roads, but the crooked roads without Improvement are roads of Genius.

Sooner murder an infant in its cradle than nurse unacted desires.

Where man is not nature is barren.

Truth can never be told so as to be understood, and not be believ'd.

Opposition is true Friendship.

One Law for the Lion & Ox is Oppression.

For everything that lives is Holy.

Enough! or Too much!

Thel's Motto

Does the Eagle know what is in the pit?
Or wilt thou go ask the Mole:
Can Wisdom be put in a silver rod?
Or Love in a golden bowl?

One Law for the Lion & Ox is Oppression

To the Muses

Whether on Ida's shady brow,
  Or in the chambers of the East,
The chambers of the sun, that now
  From antient melody have ceas'd;

Whether in Heav'n ye wander fair,
  Or the green corners of the earth,
Or the blue regions of the air,
  Where the melodious winds have birth;

Whether on chrystal rocks ye rove,
  Beneath the bosom of the sea
Wand'ring in many a coral grove,
  Fair Nine, forsaking Poetry!

How have you left the antient love
  That bards of old enjoy'd in you!
The languid strings do scarcely move!
  The sound is forc'd, the notes are few!

When a Man has Married a Wife
  he finds out whether
Her knees & elbows are only
  glued together.

Hail Matrimony, made of Love,
To thy wide gates how great a drove
On purpose to be yok'd do come:
Widows & maids & Youths also,
That lightly trip on beauty's toe
Or sit on beauty's bum.

Hail fingerfooted lovely Creatures,
The females of our human Natures
Formed to suckle all Mankind;
'Tis you that come in time of need:
Without you we should never Breed,
Or any Comfort find.

For if a Damsel's blind or lame,
Or Nature's hand has crooked her frame,
Of if she's deaf or is wall eyed:
Yet if her heart is well inclined
Some tender lover she shall find
That panteth for a Bride.

The universal Poultice, this,
To cure whatever is amiss
In damsel or in Widow gay.
It makes them smile, it makes them skip;
Like Birds just cured of the pip
They chirp & hop away.

Then come, ye Maidens, come, ye Swains,
Come & be eased of all your pains
In Matrimony's Golden cage.

The eternal gates' terrific porter lifted the northern bar:
Thel enter'd in & saw the secrets of the land unknown;
She saw the couches of the dead, & where the fibrous
      roots
Of every heart on earth infixes deep its restless twists:
A land of sorrows & of tears where never smile was
      seen.

She wander'd in the land of clouds thro' valleys dark,
      list'ning
Dolours & lamentations: waiting oft beside a dewy
      grave
She stood in silence, list'ning to the voices of the
      ground,
Till to her own grave plot she came, & there she sat
      down,
And heard this voice of sorrow breathed from the
      hollow pit:

Why cannot the Ear be closed to its own destruction?
Or the glist'ning Eye to the poison of a smile?
Why are Eyelids stor'd with arrows ready drawn,
Where a thousand fighting men in ambush lie?
Or an Eye of gifts & graces, show'ring fruits & coined
      gold?
Why a Tongue impress'd with honey from every wind?
Why an Ear, a whirlpool fierce to draw creations in?
Why a Nostril wide, inhaling terror, trembling &
      affright?
Why a tender curb upon the youthful burning boy?
Why a little curtain of flesh on the bed of our desire?

The Crystal Cabinet

The Maiden caught me in the Wild,
Where I was dancing merrily:
She put me into her Cabinet,
And Lock'd me up with a golden Key.

This Cabinet is form'd of Gold
And Pearl & Crystal shining bright,
And within it opens into a World,
And a little lovely Moony Night.

Another England there I saw,
Another London with its Tower,
Another Thames & other Hills
And another pleasant Surrey Bower.

Another Maiden like herself,
Translucent, lovely, shining clear,
Threefold each in the other clos'd:
O what a pleasant trembling fear!

O what a smile, a threefold Smile,
Fill'd me that like a flame I burn'd:
I bent to Kiss the lovely Maid,
And found a Threefold Kiss return'd.

I strove to sieze the inmost Form,
With ardor fierce & hands of flame,
But burst the Crystal Cabinet
And like a Weeping Babe became:

A weeping Babe upon the wild,
And Weeping Woman pale reclin'd;
And in the outward air again
I fill'd with woes the passing Wind.

To Thomas Butts, 16 August 1803

O why was I born with a different face,
Why was I not born like the rest of my race?
When I look each one starts! when I speak I offend,
Then I'm silent & passive & lose every Friend:

Then my verse I dishonour, my pictures despise,
My person degrade & my temper chastise,
And the pen is my terror, the pencil my shame,
All my Talents I bury, and dead is my Fame.

I am either too low or too highly priz'd
When Elate I am Envy'd, when Meek I'm despis'd.

Mock on, Mock on Voltaire, Rousseau:
Mock on, Mock on: 'tis all in vain!
You throw the sand against the wind,
And the wind blows it back again.

And every sand becomes a Gem
Reflected in the beams divine;
Blown back they blind the mocking Eye,
But still in Israel's paths they shine.

The Atoms of Democritus
And Newton's Particles of light
Are sands upon the Red sea shore,
Where Israel's tents do shine so bright.

Auguries of Innocence

To see a World in a Grain of Sand
And a Heaven in a Wild Flower,
Hold Infinity in the palm of your hand
And Eternity in an hour.
A Robin Red breast in a Cage
Puts all Heaven in a Rage.
A dove house fill'd with doves & Pigeons
Shudders Hell thro' all its regions.
A dog starv'd at his Master's Gate
Predicts the ruin of the State.
A Horse misus'd upon the Road
Calls to Heaven for Human blood.
Each outcry of the hunted Hare
A fibre from the Brain does tear.
A Skylark wounded in the wing,
A Cherubim does cease to sing.
The Game Cock clip'd & arm'd for fight
Does the Rising Sun affright.
Every Wolf's & Lion's howl
Raises from Hell a Human Soul.
The wild deer wand'ring here & there
Keeps the Human Soul from Care.
The Lamb misus'd breeds Public strife
And yet forgives the Butcher's Knife.
The Bat that flits at close of Eve
Has left the Brain that won't Believe.
The Owl that calls upon the Night
Speaks the Unbeliever's fright.

He who shall hurt the little Wren
Shall never be belov'd by Men.
He who the Ox to wrath has mov'd
Shall never be by Woman lov'd.
The wanton Boy that kills the Fly
Shall feel the Spider's enmity.
He who torments the Chafer's sprite
Weaves a Bower in endless Night.
The Catterpiller on the Leaf
Repeats to thee thy Mother's grief.
Kill not the Moth nor Butterfly,
For the Last Judgment draweth nigh.
He who shall train the Horse to War
Shall never pass the Polar Bar.
The Begger's Dog & Widow's Cat,
Feed them & thou wilt grow fat.
The Gnat that sings his Summer's song
Poison gets from Slander's tongue.
The poison of the Snake & Newt
Is the sweat of Envy's Foot.
The Poison of the Honey Bee
Is the Artist's Jealousy.
The Prince's Robes & Beggar's Rags
Are Toadstools on the Miser's Bags.
A truth that's told with bad intent
Beats all the Lies you can invent.
It is right it should be so;
Man was made for Joy & Woe;
And when this we rightly know
Thro' the World we safely go.

Joy & Woe are woven fine,
A Clothing for the Soul divine;
Under every grief & pine
Runs a joy with silken twine.
The Babe is more than swadling Bands;
Throughout all these Human Lands
Tools were made, & Born were hands,
Every Farmer Understands.
Every Tear from Every Eye
Becomes a Babe in Eternity;
This is caught by Females bright
And return'd to its own delight.
The Bleat, the Bark, Bellow & Roar
Are Waves that Beat on Heaven's Shore,
The Babe that weeps the Rod beneath
Writes Revenge in realms of death.
The Beggar's Rags, fluttering in Air,
Does to Rags the Heavens tear.
The Soldier, arm'd with Sword & Gun,
Palsied strikes the Summer's Sun.
The poor Man's Farthing is worth more
Than all the Gold on Afric's Shore.
One Mite wrung from the Lab'rer's hands
Shall buy & sell the Miser's Lands:
Or, if protected from on high,
Does that whole Nation sell & buy.
He who mocks the Infant's Faith
Shall be mock'd in Age & Death.
He who shall teach the Child to Doubt
The rotting Grave shall ne'er get out.

HELL
Canto 19

He who respects the Infant's faith
Triumphs over Hell & Death.
The Child's Toys & the Old Man's Reasons
Are the Fruits of the Two seasons.
The Questioner who sits so sly
Shall never know how to Reply.
He who replies to words of Doubt
Doth put the Light of Knowledge out.
The Strongest Poison ever known
Came from Caesar's Laurel Crown.
Nought can deform the Human Race
Like to the Armour's iron brace.
When Gold & Gems adorn the Plow
To peaceful Arts shall Envy Bow.
A Riddle or the Cricket's Cry
Is to Doubt a fit Reply.
The Emmet's Inch & Eagle's Mile
Make Lame Philosophy to smile.
He who Doubts from what he sees
Will ne'er Believe, do what you Please.
If the Sun & Moon should doubt,
They'd immediately Go out.
To be in a Passion you Good may do,
But no Good if a Passion is in you.
The Whore & Gambler, by the State
Licenc'd, build that Nation's Fate.
The Harlot's cry from Street to Street
Shall weave Old England's winding Sheet.
The Winner's Shout, the Loser's Curse,
Dance before dead England's Hearse.

Every Night & every Morn
Some to Misery are Born.
Every Morn & every Night
Some are Born to sweet delight.
Some are Born to sweet delight,
Some are Born to Endless Night.
We are led to Believe a Lie
When we see not Thro' the Eye
Which was Born in a Night to perish in a Night
When the Soul Slept in Beams of Light.
God Appears & God is Light
To those poor Souls who dwell in Night.
But does a Human Form Display
To those who Dwell in Realms of day.

And did those feet in ancient time
Walk upon England's mountains green?
And was the holy Lamb of God
On England's pleasant pastures seen?

And did the Countenance Divine
Shine forth upon our clouded hills?
And was Jerusalem builded here
Among these dark Satanic Mills?

Bring me my Bow of burning gold:
Bring me my Arrows of desire:
Bring me my Spear: O clouds unfold!
Bring me my Chariot of fire.

I will not cease from Mental Fight,
Nor shall my Sword sleep in my hand
Till we have built Jerusalem
In England's green & pleasant Land.

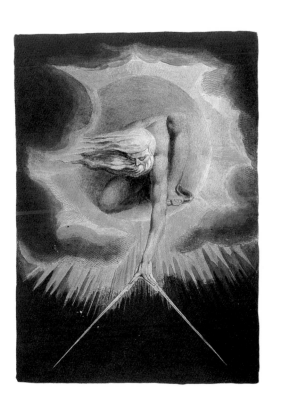

The Vision of Christ that thou dost see
Is my Vision's Greatest Enemy:
Thine has a great hook nose like thine,
Mine has a snub nose like to mine;
Thine is the friend of All Mankind,
Mine speaks in parables to the Blind;
Thine loves the same world that mine hates,
Thy Heaven doors are my Hell Gates;
Socrates taught what Melitus
Loath'd as a Nation's bitterest Curse,
And Caiphas was in his own Mind
A benefactor to Mankind.
Both read the Bible day & night,
But thou read'st black where I read white.

Advice of the Popes who Succeeded the Age of Rafael

Degrade first the Arts if you'd Mankind degrade,
Hire Idiots to Paint with cold light & hot shade:
Give high Price for the worst, leave the best in
    disgrace,
And with Labours of Ignorance fill every place.

.   .   .   .   .

When Sir Joshua Reynolds died
All Nature was degraded;
The King drop'd a tear into the Queen's Ear,
And all his Pictures Faded.

Mutual forgiveness of each Vice,
Such are the Gates of Paradise.
Against the Accuser's chief desire,
Who walked among the Stones of Fire.
Jehovah's Finger Wrote the Law
Then Wept! then rose in Zeal & Awe,
And the Dead Corpse from Sinai's heat
Buried beneath his Mercy Seat.
O Christians, Christians, tell me Why
You rear it on your Altars high?

To the Accuser Who Is the God of this World

Truly, My Satan, thou art but a Dunce,
And dost not know the Garment from the Man!
Every Harlot was a Virgin once,
Nor canst thou ever change Kate into Nan.

Tho' thou art Worship'd by the Names Divine
Of Jesus & Jehovah: thou art still
The Son of Morn in weary Night's decline,
The lost Traveller's Dream under the Hill.

NOTES ON THE POEMS

p.33 'Proverbs of Hell' from *The Marriage of Heaven and Hell*.

p.38 'Thel's Motto' from *The Book of Thel*.

p.41 'Hail Matrimony made of Love' from 'An Island in the Moon'.

p.43 'The eternal gates' terrific porter lifted the northern bar' from *The Book of Thel*, part IV.

p.54 'And did those feet in ancient time' from *Milton*.

p.56 'The Vision of Christ that thou dost see' from 'The Everlasting Gospel'.

pp.58 and 59 'Mutual forgiveness of each Vice' and 'To the Accuser Who Is the God of this World' from 'For the Sexes: The Gates of Paradise'.

NOTES ON THE PICTURES

p.6 *As if an Angel Dropped down from the Clouds*, 1809. Pen and water-colour.
Reproduced by permission of the Trustees of the British Museum, London. Photo: Bridgeman Art Library, London.

p.15 Title page to *Songs of Innocence*, 1794.
Reproduced by permission of the Trustees of the British Museum, London.

p.19 *Spring*, from *Songs of Innocence*, 1794.
Reproduced by permission of the Trustees of the British Museum, London.

p.23 Frontispiece to *Songs of Experience*, 1789–94.
Library of Congress, Washington. Photo: Bridgeman Art Library, London.

p.27 *The Tyger* from *Songs of Experience*, 1789–94.
Library of Congress, Washington. Photo: Bridgeman Art Library, London.

p.30 *A Poison Tree*, from *Songs of Experience*, 1789–94.
Library of Congress, Washington. Photo: Bridgeman Art Library, London.

p.34 *The Proverbs of Hell* from *The Marriage of Heaven and Hell*, c. 1790–3.
Reproduced by permission of the Syndics of the Fitzwilliam Museum, Cambridge.

p.39 *A Memorable Fancy* from *The Marriage of Heaven and Hell*, c. 1790–3 (detail of *Nebuchadnezzar*).
Reproduced by permission of the Syndics of the Fitzwilliam Museum, Cambridge.

p.42 *The River of Life*, c. 1805. Pen and watercolour.
Reproduced by permission of the Trustees of the Tate Gallery, London.

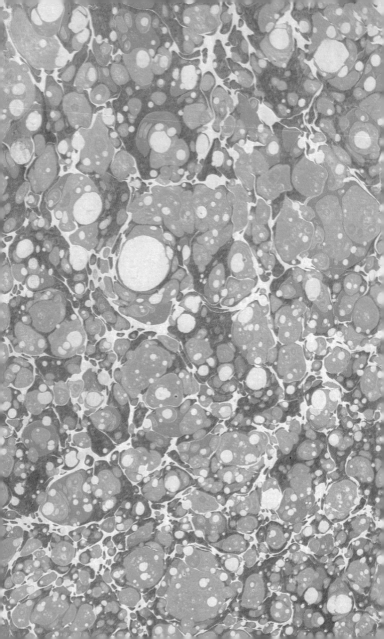